# *Real* Fitness

## 101 Games and to Get Girls Going!

### Illustrated by Carol Yoshizumi

✫ American Girl™

Published by Pleasant Company Publications

Copyright © 2006 by American Girl, LLC

Questions or comments? Call 1-800-845-0005,
visit our Web site at **americangirl.com**, or write to Customer Service,
American Girl, 8400 Fairway Place, Middleton, WI 53562-0497.

Printed in China

06 07 08 09 10 11 12 C&C 10 9 8 7 6 5 4 3 2 1

American Girl™ and its associated logos are trademarks of American Girl, LLC.

Editorial Development: Sara Hunt, Sarah Yates, Jessica Hastreiter, Mary Richards

Art Direction: Camela Decaire, Chris David, Julie Mierkiewicz

Design: Camela Decaire

Production: Kendra Schluter, Mindy Rappe, Jeannette Bailey, Judith Lary

Illustrations: Carol Yoshizumi

Special thanks to consultants Catherine Cram, Comprehensive Fitness Consulting,
and Helen Cordes, Editor, *Daughters* newsletter.

Photography: cover, p. 20—PictureQuest; p. 1, 82 (jump rope)—PictureQuest; p. 4, 8 (tying shoes)—© White Cross Productions/Getty Images; p. 4, 80 (basketball)—© Blasius Erlinger/zefa/Corbis; p. 5, 47—Thomas Heinser; p. 7—© Simon Watson/Getty Images; p. 9—Corbis; p. 11—Getty Images; p.12—© Franco Vogt/Corbis; p. 15—Getty Images; p. 19—Getty Images; p. 23—© Chris Cole/Getty Images; p. 27—© Altrendo Images/Getty Images; p. 29—Fotosearch; p. 31—Getty Images: p. 32—© Bill Deering/Getty Images; p. 33—© Matthew Murray/Getty Images; p. 34, 37—© Julia Smith/Getty Images; p. 38—© Antonio Mo/Getty Images; p. 41—Thomas Heinser; p. 43—Jim Jordan; p. 44—Monica Skeisvoll; p. 48, 51—Thomas Heinser; p. 53—© Maureen Lawrence/Getty Images; p. 54—Jim Jordan; p. 59—Monica Skeisvoll; p. 60, 63—Jim Jordan; p. 65—PictureQuest; p. 67—© Tony Anderson/Getty Images; p. 69—Corbis; p. 72—© Terry Vine/Corbis; p. 73—(laundry, vacuuming) Corbis, (cleaning supplies) Comstock Images; p. 74—(seedling) © Photolibrary.com/Getty Images, (stairs) Corbis, (watering can) © Brigitte Sporrer/zefa/Corbis; p. 75—Fotosearch; p. 77—© Bob Scott/Getty Images; p. 78—© VEER Steven Puetzer/Getty Images; p. 82—(hopscotch)© Ebby May/Getty Images; p. 83—(tennis)Corbis, (hurdles)—© Alistair Berg/Getty Images; p. 85—© Brad Wilson/Getty Images; p. 88—© Brooke Slezak/Getty Images; p. 91—© Ronnie Kaufman/Corbis

Cataloging-in-Publication Data available from Library of Congress.

# Dear Reader,

**Fitness.** You hear that buzzword everywhere these days. On the news. In health or gym class. You even read about it on your cereal box. But what is "fitness" really?

Health experts now say that girls your age should get at least one hour of physical activity every day. And, at least 3 times a week, you should try to do an activity that really gets your heart pumping for at least 30 minutes.

You don't have to play organized sports to be physically active. Simply doing two 15-minute or three 10-minute bursts of activity will provide the same health benefits as a 30-minute workout.

Your gym class counts. Extracurricular sports count. But so does recess, walking the dog—even vacuuming your bedroom. The secret is to turn off the TV, log off the computer, take a break from video games . . . and get moving!

Turn the pages of this book to find 101 steps in the right direction.

## Your friends at American Girl

# contents

## fitness facts . . . 6

From warm-up to stretching—
everything you need to know
before you get going!

## on the playground . . . 14

Learn 17 new recess games to keep you and
your friends busy at school.

## around town . . . 28

Search for activities to do
in your town in expected—
and unexpected—places.

## water games . . . 40

**12 hot ideas for staying active—and cool— on warm summer days.**

## at the pool . . . 52

**Give Marco Polo the day off. Pick from 14 new games to play in the water.**

## inside . . . 64

**Turn off your TV, log off your computer, and groove to your own tune.**

## in the yard . . . 76

**Give new meaning to the phrase "play outside." Includes backyard fun for nighttime, wintertime— anytime. You won't want to come in for dinner!**

# fitness facts

**1.** Physical activity helps make your bones, heart, and muscles stronger.

**2.** Girls who are physically active tend to sleep better and are less likely to have health problems.

**3.** Being active also helps to reduce stress, boost self-confidence, and improve thinking ability.

# Warm Up

Be sure to gently warm up for at least 5 minutes before physical activity. Try doing 5 to 8 minutes of slow walking or biking, or do one of these simple warm-ups: step side to side in place, do slow jumping jacks, or march in a small circle.

Whatever you choose as your warm-up, start out nice and easy, then slowly increase your intensity to get your body ready to get moving!

# Play It Safe

Here are some important fitness safety tips:

- Remember to drink water before, during, and after physical activity. On hot summer days, fill a water bottle halfway with water and freeze. Before you go out, fill it the rest of the way with water. You'll have cool water to sip as you go.

- Wear sunscreen outdoors. If sunscreen bothers your eyes, wear a hat or cap and apply sunscreen from your cheeks down. Don't forget to cover the back of your neck and any other exposed area of skin. Reapply often if you're swimming or sweating.

- Wear comfortable shoes.

- Wear a properly fitted helmet when appropriate. The strap should sit snugly under your chin—without pinching!

- Take it easy at first, and then slowly increase activity. If any activity causes pain or discomfort, stop. Check with your parent or doctor to make sure you're O.K.

- Swim only at pools that have appropriate supervision or a lifeguard.

- Talk to a parent to make sure it's O.K. before you go somewhere or try something new.

# Heart Pumpers

**Aerobic exercise** is any activity that gets your heart beating faster and quickens your breathing. Examples of aerobic exercise are:

**Jumping rope**

**Running**

## Dancing

**Inline skating**

**Biking**

# Playing soccer

**Swimming**

## Fitness walking

How can you tell if an activity is active enough? While you're doing it, you should be breathing too hard to sing but able to talk fairly easily.

Give your heart and lungs an aerobic workout every day to make them stronger and better able to do their job—delivering oxygen to your body!

# Bone Builders

Weight-bearing, or impact-type, physical activity involves your feet, legs, and arms supporting or carrying your body weight. Here are some activities that help to build strong bones:

Tennis

Hopscotch

Hiking

Basketball

Push-ups

Volleyball

Stair climbing

Soccer

Martial arts

## Mix it up!

Do a mix of weight-bearing and non-weight-bearing activities. Examples of non-weight-bearing activities include swimming, biking, and skateboarding.

# S-t-r-e-t-c-h

When you finish an activity, you can cool down by repeating your warm-up routine (page 8). It helps to gently stretch the muscles you've used. Try these stretches:

**Arm circles.** With your arms held straight out from your shoulders, make small circles with your arms, gradually increasing the size of the circles.

**Arm stretch.** Put your hands behind your head with your elbows out and stretch from side to side.

**Leg stretch.** Sit on the floor with your legs out in front of you. Bending from your hips, reach forward toward your feet and hold (you can bend your knees if you need to).

**Total body stretch.** Kneel on the floor, sit back on your heels, and place your arms on the floor in front of you. Press your arms down into the floor as you stretch from side to side.

**With any stretches,** remember to go slowly, and stop when you feel muscle tightness. Exhale as you stretch and inhale as you relax. Never force a stretch or continue when it hurts.

# on the playground

Get a group of friends together and get moving at recess. Pick something new to do each day, especially on days when you don't have a regular physical education class.

# 1

Hold a **jump-rope marathon** for all your friends. See who can jump the **longest,** who can do **double Dutch,** and who can turn the rope **twice** on one jump.

# 2

## Try this jump-rope trick!

Get your friends together and try jumping one rope. The tallest girl holds an adult-sized jump rope and begins jumping. Others can join one at a time to form a jumping line in front of the girl twirling the rope. To get close, a jumper can put her hands on the shoulders of the girl in front of her, but don't press down!

# 3

# Rope Relay

**You'll need:**

A rope, about 11 feet long
4 or more players, divided into 2 teams

Have 2 people hold opposite ends of the rope and spin it in a big circle.

On "Go," one player from each team runs through the rope at the same time. The player may run straight through or hop in the middle—it's up to each team to decide.

Each team tries to get its members through the moving rope. If one person touches the rope—even with her hair—her team starts over. The first team to get all its members through wins. Be sure to give the rope turners a chance to play, too!

## 4 Play Pickle

**You will need:**
**2 fielders • 2 runners • 1 tennis ball**
**4 bases or towels (sweatshirts will do!)**

Set up bases as for kickball. Each runner stands on a base. When she's ready, she dashes for an open base, trying to get there before a fielder can tag her out. If she doesn't think she can make it, she can run back to her base, where she's "safe." The fielders throw the ball back and forth to each other, trying to tag out the runners.

Runners keep track of how many bases they steal. When a runner is tagged out, she switches places with the fielder who tagged her. The first player to steal 10 bases wins.

## 5 Frisbee Fanatics

**Use a Frisbee instead of a ball to play modified versions of football, baseball, and soccer.**

# 6

**Decide on an obstacle course** and see how quickly you can get through it. Go across the monkey bars, run to the swings and pump your legs back and forth 20 times, run up the stairs to the slide, go down the slide, and do 20 jumping jacks. **Challenge your friends, too!**

# 7 Six-Legged Monster

**Line up in teams of 3. On "Go," the first and last persons in each line start stepping with their right feet, and the middle person steps with her left foot. Try to keep in step while using alternate feet, and make your way across the playground. After you practice, challenge other 6-legged monsters to a race!**

# Rings 'n' Things

Players divide up and form 2 circles.
One circle is larger than the other, and the
smaller circle is inside the larger circle.
Members of the outer circle face out,
and inner circle members face in. Players
hold hands with the others in their circle.
Select one player in the inner circle
to be the captain.

The captain directs the team through
a predetermined course by giving verbal
instructions: "Anna, go to your right.
Bridget, back up three steps." Players can
move only when the captain tells them to.
The game is over when the entire team
makes it across the finish line.

# 9 Team Tag

**Players lie on their stomachs, side by side with a partner.** The pairs of players line up to form a large circle on the ground **(like a clock), with their heads toward the center. One player is It, and another player starts the game by running up to a pair and lying down next to one of the partners before being tagged by It.**

**The partner on the other side of that pair must then get up and run and find a new spot, again while trying not to be tagged by It. If the person who is It tags the runner, they reverse roles.**

# 10
# Scream Team

Line up side by side along one end of a big field. On "Go," **each player yells as loudly** as she can **while she runs** toward the opposite side of the field. Here's the catch—you may **run only as long as you can yell!** When you run out of breath, stop. See who can go the farthest—and scream the loudest!

## Kitty Corner

# 11

You need 5 players to play this game. Four people make a square with one person at each corner. The fifth person stands in the middle. She is "Kitty"—she wants a corner, too! The object of the game is to change places without letting Kitty get a corner. When Kitty yells "Change!" all the players scramble to change corners. As they change, Kitty tries to run to an empty corner. Whoever is left without a corner becomes Kitty.

# 12

## Monkey in the Middle

One person is the Monkey and she sits on a stool or on the ground in the center of a circle. The other players run, skip, or dance around the Monkey, chanting "Monkey in the middle, you can't catch me!" The Monkey has to try to catch someone without leaving her stool (or spot). The person who's caught becomes the next Monkey.

## Rainbow Tag 13

Choose a home base. One player is It. The other players are the Rainbow. They each think of a color to be—without saying their color out loud. The person who is It calls out a color. When a player's color is called, she runs for the base and It tries to catch her. If she reaches the base without getting tagged, she chooses another color and rejoins the rainbow. If she is caught, she's out.

## 14 Wagon Wheel

Draw a huge wagon wheel with chalk on the blacktop or concrete. First make a circle about 25 feet wide. Then make 8 spokes across it. One player is It. She chases the other players up and down the spokes and around the outside of the circle. When someone is tagged, she becomes It. Try it. It's wheel-y fun!

# Ribbon Row

All the players but one stand in a single-file row or line. Each player puts her hands on the shoulders of the player in front of her to make a "ribbon." The player not in the ribbon is It. She tries to catch the last person in the ribbon, while the ribbon twists and turns (and runs!) to get away. When It finally tags the last person on the ribbon, she puts her hands on that girl's shoulders, and the girl at the front of the ribbon becomes It.

# 16

Watch where you step with this game of tag. Use chalk to outline two pairs of feet. You're "safe" only when you stand in the chalk feet.

# 17

Grab a pal and draw a big **tic-tac-toe board** with chalk. In each square, write a different exercise—8 push-ups, 20 toe touches, and so on. You must complete the exercise to get an X or O in that square.

# around town

There are so many things to do in your town. With many of them, you won't even know you're improving your fitness. Check your local yellow pages for ideas.

# 18

## Have a Sca-venture!

**Go on a scavenger hunt adventure through your neighborhood or a local park or trail. Along the way, try to locate each of the things listed on the next page. Take pictures or just make a checklist, since you can't bring the items home with you. Gather small leaves and flowers or other items to make a collage when you get home!**

1. **A leafy tree**
2. **A green trash can**
3. **Swings**
4. **Someone wearing sneakers**
5. **A pretty rock**
6. **A dog**
7. **A baby stroller (or baby)**
8. **A blue car**
9. **A fire hydrant**
10. **A U.S.P.S. mailbox (or mail truck)**

# 19 Pick berries at a local fruit farm. Be sure to sample some fresh sweetness after you pick!

# 20 Visit a local farmers' market.
As you walk around, look for fresh ingredients to make something healthy and delicious when you get home.

# 21

## Go to the zoo

**and take photos of animals—
from anteater to zebra—to
make an A-to-Z book for a
child you know (such as
a younger sibling, cousin,
or neighbor).**

**22** Collect seashells on the beach to use in a craft project.

**23** Walk around the mall with friends (no stopping for shopping!). Wear a pedometer to count your steps.

**24** Need a new book? **Walk or bike** to the local library.

**25** **Organize a** family hike or bike ride. **Take turns being the leader or tour guide. Pack a picnic lunch, and stop to eat it along the way.**

**26** **Go on a brisk walk** with a parent or friend. Choose a route that has lots of hills. Mix it up! Walk 2 minutes. Run 2 minutes. Skip 2 minutes. Hop 2 minutes. Tiptoe 2 minutes. Repeat.

**27** Time how long it takes you to run around your house or the block. Rest 2 minutes. Run again and try to improve your time.

If you have a friend in the neighborhood, walk to her house. If she comes to your house, walk her home (at least halfway). **28**

**29** Push a younger sibling or neighbor around the neighborhood in a stroller. Or push her on the swing.

Clean up the neighborhood. Take a trash bag and pick up the litter on your street or in your parks. It's a good idea to wear rubber gloves if you'll be handling trash. **30**

# 31 Take your dog for a run—not a walk.

**32** Get a group together to play **miniature golf** or go **bowling.**

**33** Check out an indoor **rock-climbing** facility.

**34** Find out about **open gym times** and activities at your local gym.

**35** Head to your nearest **ice-skating** or **roller-skating** rink.

**36** Other nearby spots to ask about: **play mazes, ball pits,** and **batting cages**

# water games

Get wet and cool off!
Play these games in your
backyard on a hot summer day.
Invite some friends over and
put on your swimsuits.
Then just add water!

## 37 Duck, Duck, Fish

Play Duck, Duck, Goose in the usual way, except that the Goose is a Fish. To pick the Fish, dump a cup of water on her head.

## 38 Sopping-Wet Tag

Wet a sponge thoroughly and throw it to tag players.

# Splash— you're It!

# 39 Sprinkler Skip

Have everyone stand in a circle and jump over the spray of a rotating sprinkler. If you get wet, you're out. The girl who stays dry the longest is the winner!

# 40 Walk This Way

Have players divide into 2 teams and line up. Set a bucketful of water in front of each team and an empty bucket about 10 yards away. Give the first person in each line a paper cup. On "Go," she has to fill her cup with water from the bucket, balance the cup on her head, and walk or run to the empty bucket to dump the water. She runs back and hands the cup to the next person in line. The relay continues for 2 minutes. Whichever team has more water in its bucket at the end wins!

# 41 On Guard

Place 2 piles of 10 water balloons in the yard. Divide into 2 teams. Each team has to guard its water balloons but must also try to steal the other team's water balloons. See which team has more unbroken balloons after 3 minutes!

# 42
## Squish Relay

Divide into 2 teams. Fill enough water balloons so that each person has 7 or 8. Each player must race across the yard to the finish line with as many water balloons as she can hold. The trick? No hands are allowed! If a balloon pops, the player must start over. The first team to finish wins!

# 43
## Swinkler

Set up a sprinkler in front of a swing.

# Wheeeee!

# 44 Volleyballoon

**Two players stand on each side of a volleyball net, holding a towel between them.** They serve a water balloon to the other side by placing it in the towel and launching it over the net. The players on the other side must catch the balloon in their towel and then launch it back. If the balloon breaks on your team's side, the other team gets a point. If a team launches the balloon out-of-bounds, the other team gets a point. Play to 10.

# 45
## No-ball Fight

**Have a warm-weather snowball fight!** Divide into teams, fill a couple of buckets with water, and give each team a pile of clean sponges. Players throw wet sponges at the other team. If you get hit, you're out. The first team to run out of players loses.

# 46
## Splash Tag

**Stand across from a friend, and toss a water balloon back and forth until it pops and splashes one of you. The person who gets splashed has to chase the other person until she tags her.**

## 47 Save the Soda

Each player gets 3 sponges and an empty 2-liter soda bottle. Set up the bottles on the ground. Each player tries to protect her own bottle while trying to knock down the other players' bottles with the sponges. The player with the last standing bottle wins!

## 48 Splat Bat

Pitch a friend a few water balloons for some wet and wild batting practice!

# at the pool

Head to your local swimming pool and try these original pool games. Invite someone you've never played with before to play, too. Remember to reapply sunscreen after swimming.

# 49

# In Sync

**Get your friends together and choreograph a synchro-nized swimming routine. Invite parents and siblings to watch the final performance. Encore, encore!**

## Make a Splash

Try this routine with a friend! Practice on deck first. To stay on the beat, play some music. Here's a tip: Glance at each other out of the corners of your eyes to make sure your arms move the same way at the same time.

- Lift right arm over head and lower down to side on beats 1 and 2.
- Repeat with left arm on beats 3 and 4.
- Dive forward on beat 5. Swim underwater for beats 6 and 7.
- Come up to surface with hands up on beat 8. Ta-da!

# 50 Toss Across

Give each team 10 soft foam balls that are easily distinguished from the opponents' balls. Assign each team one end of the pool. Have one person be the timer. Each team tries to get all of its balls to the opposite end of the pool, while tossing the opposing team's balls back to them. See which team has more balls at their end of the pool after one minute.

# 51 Sky Ball

See how long you and your friends can keep a beach ball in the air without letting it hit the water.

# 52

## Roly-Poly
**Race a friend** across the pool while floating on a beach ball. If you fall off, get back on and keep going!

# 53

## Wet Sponge Relay

**Set 2 empty buckets on one side of the pool. Have players start on the other side and swim in inner tubes across the pool with sponges. Players must squeeze the sponge water into the bucket and swim back to pass the sponge to the next girl. The team that has more water in its bucket after 2 minutes wins the game.**

## 54 Use Your Noodle

Divide into 2 teams. Team 1 has a player at each base and a pitcher. Team 2 is first up to bat. Use a beach ball and pool noodle for the ball and bat. Players should swim to bases. Play for 3 innings. Batter up!

## 55 Wacky Water Relay

Divide into 2 teams. Each player on a team must swim to the end of the pool and back again while doing something different. For example, Player 1 swims with a pool noodle, Player 2 swims while pushing a beach ball, Player 3 uses an inner tube, and so on. After each girl completes her task, she must tag the next player. The first team to finish wins the race!

# 56 Splashketball

Float a hula hoop or inner tube by the edge of the pool. Each girl takes a small ball and jumps into the pool with it. While in the air, she throws the ball toward the hoop and tries to score.

# 57 Fast Grab

Collect Ping-Pong balls, small plastic soda bottles, or anything small that floats. Toss the items into a pool. Players must swim around and grab as many things as they can in 1 minute. The person with the most objects wins.

## 58 High and Dry

In this goofy swimming race, each player should be holding a tennis ball. The object is to win the race while keeping the tennis ball dry!

## 59 Aqua Obstacle

Set up an obstacle course in the pool. Pop through a hula hoop, swim under a pool noodle, and swim over a beach ball.

## 60 Poolympics

**Make up your own mini Olympics with events like noodle races and splash contests!**

## 61 Beach Ball Push

Have a race to see who can push a beach ball across the pool—with her nose—in the shortest amount of time.

## 62 Sing While You Swim!

Have a silly race! See who can swim on her back the fastest while singing a song. If a player stops singing, she needs to begin again!

# inside

Spend less than two hours a day watching television and you can't help but be more active around the house.

Turn on some tunes and move. When you're done, clean your room— it's great exercise. Really!

## Dance-a-thon

63

Pick partners and turn on some music.
Each pair puts a balloon between their foreheads.
Everyone dances (you have to keep moving!),
keeping the balloon in place with no hands.
Partners are out if they drop their balloon. The
last team dancing wins.

## Crabwalk Race

64

Set a bunch of balloons in the middle of the room.
Divide players into 2 teams. Set a timer for 2
minutes. All players must crabwalk while they try
to get as many balloons to their side of the room
as possible. The team with more balloons at the
end of 2 minutes wins.

## Balloon Ball

65

This game is a kick! One girl raises her arms
above her head to make a goal. Set a balloon
a few feet in front of her. Pick a player to try to
kick the balloon through the goal. See who
can kick the most goals.

## Knee Knocker

66

See who can walk the farthest or fastest
with a balloon held between her knees.

# Boogie Fever

## Try some fun dances from the 1960s and 1970s.

**67** **The Swim:** Hold your nose with one hand, make a swimming motion with the other, and then switch. Don't forget to swing your hips!

**68** **The Funky Chicken:** Put your hands under your armpits, flap your elbows like wings, and knock your knees together.

**69** **The Twist:** Bend your knees and swivel them to the right while you turn your torso to the left, then reverse. Once you've got the hang of it, see how long you can go!

# Get Movin' and Groovin'

## Warm-ups

Turn on some dance tunes and get yourself warmed up. Make up a dance move for each part of your body (arms, legs, head). Put them all together—and you're groovin'!

Dance video games are another great way to move to the beat. As you learn the dances, remember:

• Your feet don't always have to be moving. Simply move your hips or shoulders—you are still dancing.

• Be dramatic and exaggerate your moves. The more you groove, the more you move!

# 71
## Boogie Board

You've never danced like this before! Lie on the floor on your stomach as if you were on a boogie board. Turn on some music and dance—without letting your arms or legs touch the floor! Invite some friends over for a boogie contest. Who can boogie the longest?

# 72
## High Steps

Hold a broomstick horizontally at waist level. Lift your knee so that it touches the stick. See how many touches you can get in a minute.

## 73

### Hula-hoop

**to your favorite song. Try twirling the hoop around your waist, legs, and arms.**

## 74

### Jump rope

**to music. Try jumping side to side, backward, and with scissor legs.**

## 75

### Make up a cheerleading routine.

**Include 3 different jumps, dancing, and loud cheering. Practice until it's perfect!**

# 76
# **More** get
# *m-o-v-i-n-g* tips!

**You probably wouldn't think of
these activities as "fitness,"
but they get your heart pumping
just the same as many exercises.**

## Make your bed.

**Pretend you're working in a
hotel and you have to finish
before the guests arrive.**

## Vacuum the house.

**If you can safely carry the vacuum cleaner up and down the stairs, all the better!**

## Help with the laundry

**(especially if the laundry room is in the basement and your dirty clothes are on the floor in your room two flights upstairs)!**

## Wash windows

**(those that you can reach safely).**

# Plant or weed a garden.

**Watch it grow!**

## Take the stairs

**. . . in pairs. Use the stairs every chance you get (skip the escalator!). Try to go briskly—and skip every other step.**

# Water your grass

**and your mother's flowers. Then cool yourself off with the hose, too!**

**Babysit.** You'll be surprised how much energy you'll need to keep up with (or carry around) little kids! Take a baby-sitting course before your first job.

# in the yard

See how many of these different activities you can try—all year long.

If you have a stopwatch, time yourself doing some, then challenge yourself to improve your time. You'll get faster and fitter!

**77** **Rake leaves and jump into the piles!** Create several small piles around the yard to make a hurdle-jumping track. When the fun's done, time yourself to see how fast you can stuff the leaves into bags.

## 78 Chase fireflies.

Clean out an empty mayonnaise jar, have an adult poke holes in the lid, then go outside at dusk and see your backyard light up with fireflies. (It helps to let your grass grow longer than usual!) Divide into teams of 2 (a catcher and a jar manager). As the catcher catches a firefly, the jar manager follows up with the jar, opens it, and pops the firefly in! Watch them glow. Don't forget to set them free before bedtime.

## 79 Make your own mini golf course with clean, empty cans and boxes for the holes and a kiddie pool and sandbox as the water hazard and sand trap.

## 80 When it's hot out, offer to wash the car for your parents. Then offer to wash the neighbors' car. They'll be thrilled and you'll stay cool.

# 81

Grab a
**basketball**
and have a
**shoot-off.**

**See how many free throws you can sink in 60 seconds.**

## 82

**Play broomball** with your friends. Draw 2 goals on your driveway with chalk. Use brooms like hockey sticks to score using a tennis ball.

## 83

**Dribble a basketball while sprinting** up and down the sidewalk. Count how many bounces you can get. Try to beat your own score.

## 84

**Play tennis against the garage door.** How many times can you hit the ball against the door?

## 85

See how many times you can **bounce a tennis ball** on top of your racket without the ball hitting the ground.

# 86 Design your own obstacle course.

**Station 1:** Jump rope.

**Station 2:** Hula-hoop.

**Station 3:** Play hopscotch on the sidewalk or driveway.

**Station 4:** Balance on a board or on a line drawn with chalk on the driveway.

## Station 5:
Swing on the swings.

## Station 6:
Bounce a ball in the air 10 times on a tennis racket.

## Station 7:
Go across the monkey bars.

## Station 8:
Slide down the slide.

## Station 9:
Make a hurdle and leap to the finish line!

# Introduce a soccer ball to your feet.

**87** Use your instep to kick the ball with surprising power. Use the sole of your foot to stop the ball. Use your heel to go into reverse and pass behind you. Use the sides of your feet to make passes.

**88** Play switch-leg soccer. For 2 minutes, kick the ball only with your right foot. Then switch and kick only with your left foot.

**89** Play klutz soccer! If you are right-handed, play with your left foot only. If you are left-handed, use your right foot. It will improve your coordination, and you'll be surprised how easy things seem when you finally switch feet.

# Try one of these or design your own themed relay.

90

## Hula in a Hurry

Fill 2 separate buckets with "hula gear" such as sunglasses, beach hats, hula skirts, swimsuit tops, leis, and so on. (There can be duplicates of things to make the game more difficult.) Split into 2 teams and get into 2 lines. On "Go," one girl from each team runs to her bucket and dresses as fast as she can, putting everything on. Once she is dressed, she must yell "hula!" Then she takes off her hula gear, puts it back into the bucket, and runs to tag her teammate, who does the same thing. The first team that finishes wins.

## 91

## Backpack Relay

Fill 2 backpacks with an equal number
of camping items, such as a compass,
a flashlight, and soap. Put a map and a
teddy bear in each pack. Line up 2 teams
facing each other. On "Go," the first player
from each team puts on her pack and runs
to the other side. She unpacks her pack,
unfolds and refolds the map, kisses the
bear, and repacks the pack. Then she
runs back to her team and puts
the pack on the next player.
The first team to finish wins!

## 92 Tic-Tac-Snow

Put on your boots and play this twist on an old game. After a fresh snowfall, mark the lines of a tic-tac-toe board in the snow with your footprints. Hop from square to square to make your Xs and Os!

## 93

Shovel snow and make a snow fort out of the huge pile you make!

## 94 Get your heart pumping with a snowman race!

Get a group of 4 girls together and break into 2 teams. See which team can build a life-size snowman faster. Don't forget the face!

# 95

## Skating Signature

Try this trick the next time you go ice-skating with your friends. See if you can **spell out your name on the ice with your skates.** Try skating your initials first, and work up to your whole name. It's tricky!

# 96

# Go sledding.

**Learn how to steer, slow down, and stop your sled. When you get to the bottom of the hill, race back to the top.**

# 97

## Think of a game you enjoy during the day, and figure out a way to play it at night.

**Play volleyball with a glowing inflatable ball or add reflective tape to a soccer ball.**

# Anything is possible!

**Night Rules:** Always ask your parents before playing night games. Never play in the street. Check your yard the day before you play. Avoid holes, mud, rocks, hills, glass, etc. If you're riding your bike at night, wear reflective clothing. Make sure your bike has a headlight and a rear reflector.

# 98

## Star Struck

Play celebrity freeze tag with a flashlight. Yell out a star's name before you are tagged by the light. You can use a name only once. If the light hits you before you call out a name, freeze—you're out!

# 99

## Dance in the Spotlight!

Turn on some music and stand in a circle. One person stands in the center with a flashlight. The circle begins moving clockwise. The girl with the flashlight closes her eyes. After a few seconds, she says "Stop" and turns on the flashlight. The person in the spotlight must dance for 15 seconds. The sillier the dancing, the better! After dancing, she trades places with the girl in the center. The fun begins again!

# 100
## Star

Have one person be Star and hold a glow-in-the-dark ball. Star throws the ball into the air while yelling out a player's name (the new Star). The new Star must get the ball while all other players run away. As soon as the ball is caught, the new Star yells "star!" and all the players must freeze. Star takes 3 gigantic steps toward any player and gently throws the ball to tag her. If she tags the player, then that person becomes Star. If she misses, she is still Star.

# 101
## Glow Fetch

Use a glow-in-the-dark rubber ball or Frisbee (available at discount stores and pet stores), and play fetch with your furry friend!

## Real Fitness
# Challenge

**Keep track of which *Real Fitness*
games and activities you try.
Send us a letter to tell us
how you do!**

**Write to:**

**Real Fitness Editor
American Girl
8400 Fairway Place
Middleton, WI 53562**

# Here are some other American Girl books that you might like:

Skin & Nails
Care Tips for Girls

❑ I read it.

Hair
Styling Tips and Tricks for Girls

❑ I read it.

SPORTS and SPIRIT STUFF
secrets
Improve your skills and have more fun—in any sport!

❑ I read it.

The Care & Keeping of YOU
The Body Book for Girls

❑ I read it.

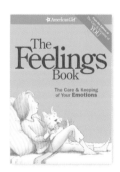

The Feelings Book
The Care & Keeping of Your Emotions

❑ I read it.